Malcolm Penny

SHARKS

Illustrated by Wendy Meadway

Language Consultant:
Diana Bentley
University of Reading

PUFFIN BOOKS

Words printed in
bold are explained
in the glossary.

Contents

Help! Sharks!

Most people are afraid of sharks, because they think that they will **attack** people who go swimming. In some parts of the world big sharks are dangerous, but there are many

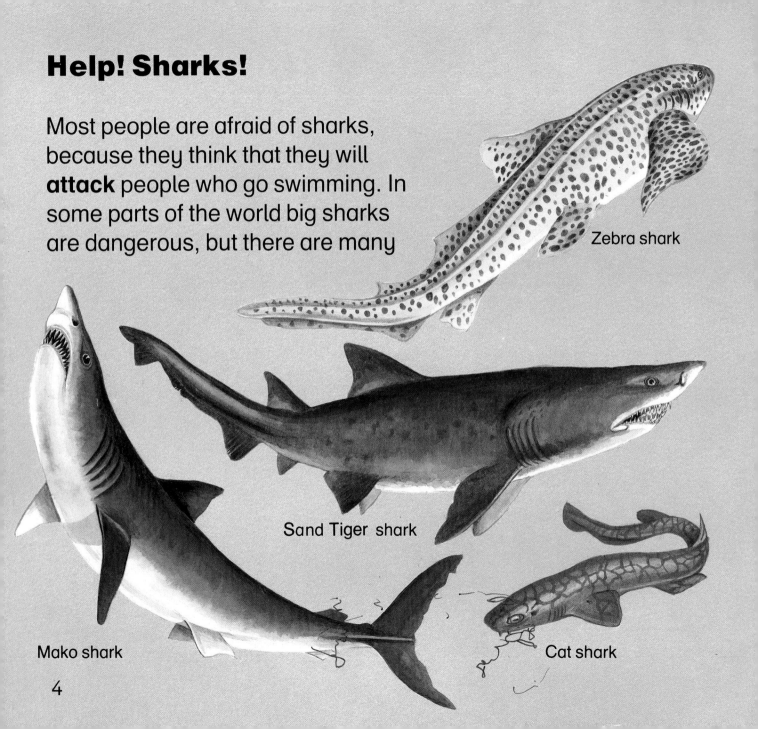

Zebra shark

Sand Tiger shark

Mako shark

Cat shark

4

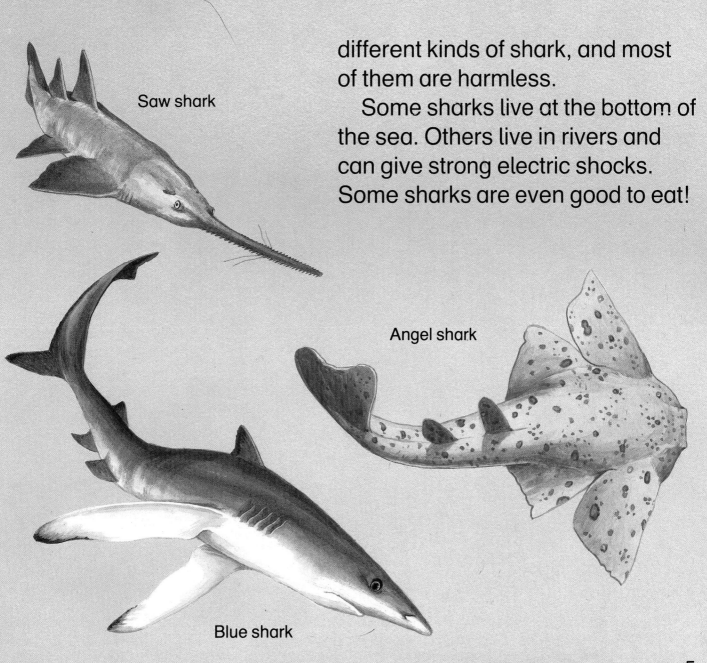

different kinds of shark, and most of them are harmless.

Some sharks live at the bottom of the sea. Others live in rivers and can give strong electric shocks. Some sharks are even good to eat!

Saw shark

Angel shark

Blue shark

What is a shark?

Sharks are fish, but they are different from fish like cod or herring because a shark has soft bones.

Tiger shark

Fin

Eye

Gill openings

Nostril

Tail

Fin

Mouth

Fins

Fins

Like other fish, they use **gills** to breathe under water. A shark's skin is very tough and covered in small **spines**. All sharks are hunters, but not all of them are fierce. Some of them only hunt snails or shrimps.

Their teeth grow in rows, so that as the front ones are worn out or broken off, new ones come forward to replace them.

Front of mouth

Looking down on rows of teeth waiting to come forward

How a shark breathes

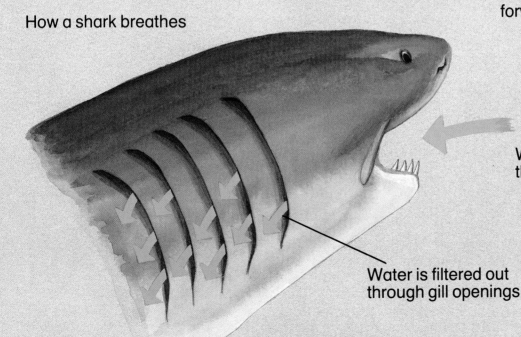

Water is taken in through the mouth

Water is filtered out through gill openings

7

The great white shark

Great white sharks are really grey
or brown on top, but they are white
underneath. They are found in
warm seas all around the world.
They can grow up to six metres long.

They have sharp, triangular teeth, and they are very fierce. Their usual food is fish, seals and dolphins, but they sometimes attack and eat people. They follow ships to eat any rubbish thrown overboard.

Thresher sharks

Thresher sharks can grow to six metres long, as big as white sharks. They use their long tails to drive smaller fish into a group to catch them.

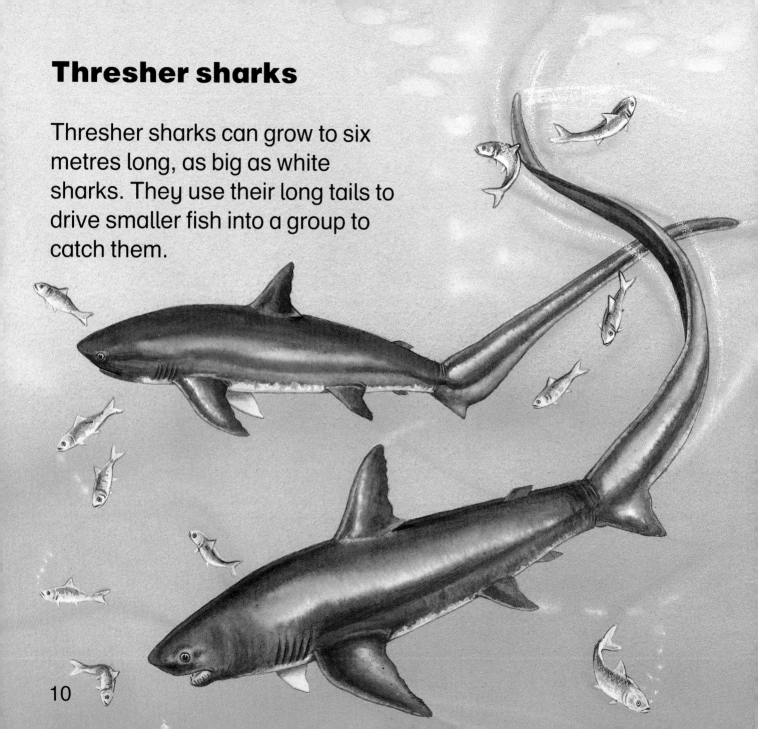

In the summer, thresher sharks may come into shallow water near the coast. During the rest of the year, they live far out to sea, in places where the water is not too cold.

Threshers with a shoal of herring

Hammerhead and whale sharks

A hammerhead shark has its eyes at the end of thick **stalks**, which makes its head look like a hammer. Hammerheads live in warm parts of the world. They often come close to the beach. They usually eat fish or squid.

Hammerhead shark

Whale shark

Whale sharks live far out in deep, warm seas. They are the biggest of all fish, and can grow to over fifteen metres long. They move slowly, and are quite harmless. They feed by straining small fish and shrimps out of the water.

The divers look very small next to the huge whale shark

13

Dogfish

Dogfish are small sharks. They are only about eighty centimetres long. They live in cool seas. They feed on the bottom of the sea, mostly on worms and shellfish.

14

The empty shells of their eggs are called 'mermaid's purses' when they are washed up on to beaches. Unlike most sharks, dogfish are good to eat. They are usually called 'rock salmon' in fish shops.

Dogfish

Rays

Rays are part of the shark family, although they are very different in shape. They are triangular, and they flap their wings to fly like birds under the water.

How a ray swims

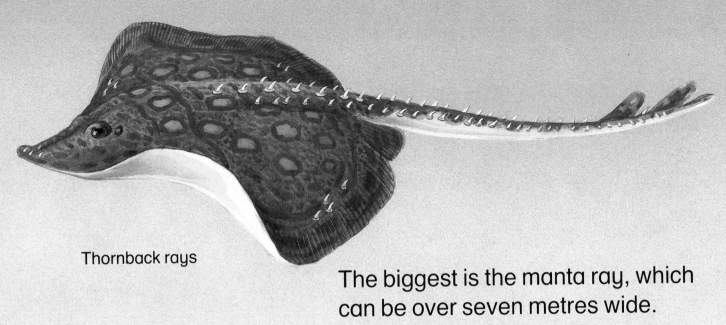

Thornback rays

The biggest is the manta ray, which can be over seven metres wide. Like the whale shark, the manta ray feeds on small fish and shrimps. Eagle rays fly together under the water in **flocks**. They dive to the bottom of the sea to find crabs and shellfish to eat.

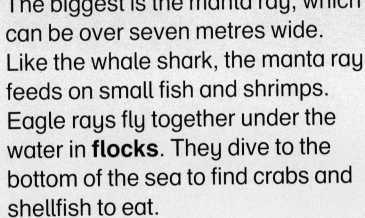

Two strange sharks

The electric ray is a very strange
member of the shark family. It lives
in rivers or very deep in the sea. It
cannot see to hunt in the muddy
water so it finds its **prey** by feeling
with its fins. Then it kills its food with
a strong electric shock.

A fish swims over a
partly-hidden electric ray

The wobbegong looks like a rug. It is sometimes called a carpet shark. It lives among **coral**, in warm shallow water. It digs up shellfish such as winkles and clams to eat.

Wobbegong shark

How sharks swim

Rays fly like birds, but the hunting sharks fly through the water like aeroplanes. Their tails sweep from side to side to drive them along, and their front fins work like stiff wings to keep them up.

Grey sharks in an aquarium

Sharks cannot float. If they stop swimming, they sink. One shark in an **aquarium** in Australia swam round its tank without stopping for four years. In that time, it travelled over 160,000 kilometres.

21

How sharks hunt

The swift hunting sharks find their prey by feeling movements in the water. They can tell if a fish or a seal is wounded or trying to escape. Sharks attack these animals.

Grey reef sharks

Sharks can also smell their prey in the water, from a long way away. When a shark attacks, it raises its head to open its mouth very wide. Then it bites and shakes its prey to cut pieces off it.

What sharks eat

All sharks eat other animals. The big hunting sharks eat seals and sea lions, dolphins and even small whales. The smaller ones eat fish or squid.

Crocodile shark feeding

Great white shark chasing a dolphin

Port Jackson shark with oysters and sea urchins

Sharks which live on the bottom of the sea eat crabs, sea snails and worms. They have blunt teeth, for crunching up shells. Did you know that the biggest sharks, like the manta ray and the whale shark, eat the smallest food!

Basking shark filtering food

Sharks and their babies

Some sharks have babies, which grow inside their mother until they are ready to be born.

A lemon shark gives birth. The diver holds one of the newly born pups

Other sharks lay eggs. The eggs have long curly strings to fix them to rocks until they hatch. The young sharks swim away in search of food. Some mother sharks do not lay their eggs, but let them hatch inside their bodies.

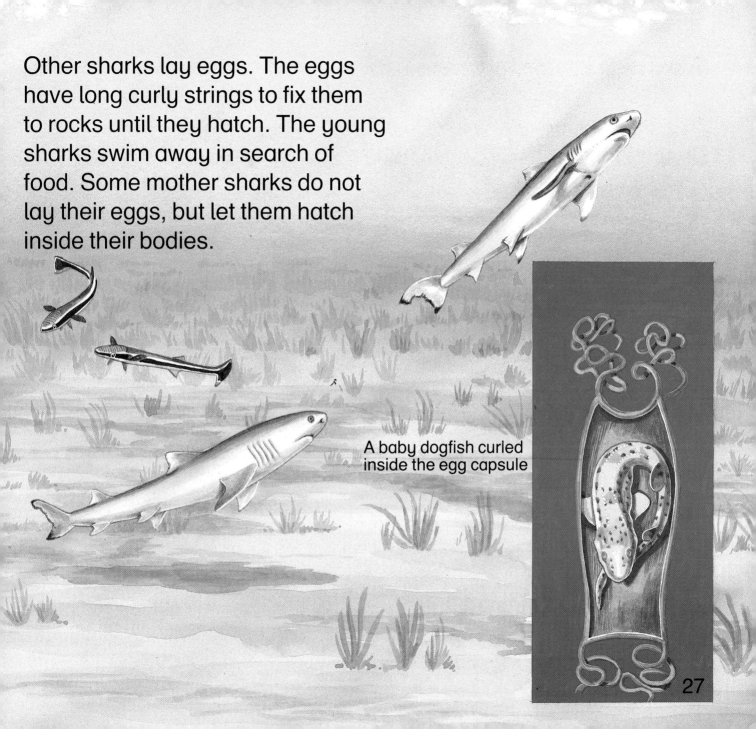

A baby dogfish curled inside the egg capsule

27

Sharks and people

Great white sharks are not the only ones that are dangerous to people. Hammerheads, blue sharks and sand sharks will all attack if they have the chance.

In warm countries, there is often a net in the sea to keep sharks away from beaches where people swim. A few small sharks, such as dogfish, are good to eat. Some Chinese people use shark fins to make a special soup.

Sharks are being studied by scientists, so that we can learn more about them.

Nets keep sharks away from swimmers on this Australian beach

Glossary

Aquarium A pool in which animals are kept so that we can go to look at them.

Attack To hurt or harm something.

Coral A growth which looks like a plant and lives on rocks and the floor of warm seas.

Flocks A large group of animals of one kind.

Gills The part of a fish through which it breathes.

Prey An animal hunted or captured by another animal for food.

Spines Hard-pointed parts of the shark's skin.

Stalks Long structures attached to the body of the shark.

Books to read

Sharks, Bernard
 Stonehouse (Wayland, 1985).
Sharks, Neil Grant
 (Hamlyn, 1985).
Sharks in the Wild, Cliff
 Moon (Wayland, 1985).
*Sharks, Whales, Dolphins
 and Seals,* Paul Frame
 (Franklin Watts, 1985).
World of Sharks, Andrew
 Langley (Wayland, 1987).

Index